T0063928

Jasmine 2.0

Jasmine 2.0

DALE ROBINSON

authorHOUSE®

AuthorHouse™ LLC
1663 Liberty Drive
Bloomington, IN 47403
www.authorhouse.com
Phone: 1-800-839-8640

© 2014 Dale Robinson. All rights reserved.

No part of this book may be reproduced, stored in a retrieval system, or transmitted by any means without the written permission of the author.

Published by AuthorHouse 12/20/2013

ISBN: 978-1-4918-5636-9 (sc)

Any people depicted in stock imagery provided by Thinkstock are models, and such images are being used for illustrative purposes only. Certain stock imagery © Thinkstock.

This book is printed on acid-free paper.

Because of the dynamic nature of the Internet, any web addresses or links contained in this book may have changed since publication and may no longer be valid. The views expressed in this work are solely those of the author and do not necessarily reflect the views of the publisher, and the publisher hereby disclaims any responsibility for them.

Table of Contents

Books that Jasmine and I read Together

Cocoa Ice by. Diana Appelbaum

Dancing In The Wings by. Debbie Allen

The Sunday Outing by. Gloria Jean Pinkney

Fox On Stage by. Edward Marshall

Jamaica Is Thankful by. Juanita Havill

Paul Robeson by. Patricia and Fredrick McKissack

Henry Aaron's Dream by. Matt Tavares

Authur's Tooth by. Marc Brown

Jamela's Dress by. Niki Daly

Fox and His Friends by. Edward Marshall

Can You See What I See by. Walter Wick

Satchel Paige by. Patricia and Fredrick McKissack

Dale Robinson

Doo Wop Pop by. Roni Schotter

The Runaway Bunny by. Margaret Brown

Marian Anderson by. Patricia and Fredrick McKissack

George Washington Carver by. Patricia and Fredrick McKissack

The Banza: A Haitian Story by. Diane Wolkstein

Jazz On A Saturday Night by. Diana Dillon

Madame C.J. Walker by. Patricia and Fredrick McKissack

Martin Luther King Jr. by. Patricia and Fredrick McKissack

The Princess and The Pizza by. Mary Auch

Beans to Chocolate by. Inez Snyder

You're My Nikki by. Phyllis Rose Eisenberg

Josias, Hold The Book by. Jennifer Riesmeyer Elvgren

Arthur Meets The President by. Marc Brown

Arthur Jumps Into Fall by. Marc Brown

Big Boy by. Tololwa M. Mollel

Clockwise by. Sara Pinto

Long Night Moon by. Cynthia Rylant

Wangari's Trees Of People by. Jeanette Winter

Full Full Full Of Love by. Trish Cooke

The Life Cycle Of A Honeybee by. Ruth Thomson

Jamaica's Find by. Juanita Havill

Zora Neale Hurston by. Patricia and Fredrick McKissack

Sojourner Truth by. Patricia and Fredrick McKissack

Ma Dear's Aprons by. Patricia McKissack

Madeline by. Ludwig Bemelmans

The True Story Of The 3 Little Pigs by. Jon Scieszka

Jesse Owens by. Patricia And Fredrick McKissack

Langston Hughes by. Patricia And Fredrick McKissack

Dora Climbs Star Mountain by. Alison Inches

Mirandy And Brother Wind by. Patricia McKissack

Arthur's Computer Disaster by. Marc Brown

Fox In Love by. Edward Marshall

Stellaluna by. Janell Cannon

Satchel Paige—"Don't Look Back" by. David A. Adler

This Car by. Paul Collicutt

Rent Party Jazz by. William Miller

Freedom Summer by. Deborah Wiles

Arthur And The True Francine by. Marc Brown

Soccer Hour by. Carol Nevius

Dizzy by. Jonah Winter

Coming Home by. Floyd Cooper

Fox Outfoxed by. James Marshall

Arthur Turns Green by. Marc Brown

Jesse Owens—"Fastest Man Alive" by. Carole Boston Weatherford

Kate, The Cat And The Moon by. David Almond & Stephen Lambert

Dale Robinson

Harvey Moon, Museum Boy by. Pat Cummings

Puddles by. Jonathan London

Ballerina Dreams by. Lauren Thompson

Bring On That Beat by. Rachel Isadora

Arthur's Underwear by. Marc Brown

Circus! by. Peter Spier's

Those Shoes by. Maribeth Boelts

Jelly Beans For Sale by. Bruce McMillan

Brianna, Jamaica And The Dance Of Spring by. Juanita Havill

My Row And Piles Of Coins by. Tololwa M. Mollel

The Sea Chest by. Toni Buzzeo

Fox At School by. Edward Marshall

Arthur's Chicken Pox by. Marc Brown

And The Dish Ran Away With The Spoon by. Janet Stevens & Susan Stevens Crummel

When Marian Sang by. Pam Munoz

My Big Brother by. Miriam Cohen

Dogs by. Gail Gibbons

If You Were An Astronaut by. Virginia Schomp

Booker T. Washington "Teacher, Speaker And Leader by. Suzanne Slade

The Race Of The Century by. Barry Downard

Joe Louis by. David A. Adler

Rosa by. Nikki Giovanni

One Million Men & Me by. Kelly Starling Lyons

Harriet Tubman—"Hero Of The Underground Railroad" by. Lori Mortensen

Just Like Josh Gibson By. Angela Johnson

Arthur's First Sleepover by. Marc Brown

Arthur's Family Vacation by. Marc Brown

Fox Be Nimble by. James Marshall

Jazzy Miz Mozetta by. Brenda C. Roberts

Arthur's Baby by. Marc Brown

Grandma Lena's Big OL 'Turnip by. Denia Lewis Hester

Jamaica And The Substitute Teacher by. Juanita Havill

Michael's Golden Rules by. Deloris Jordan

Nothing But Trouble "The Story of Althea Gibson" by. Sue Stauffacher

Kenya's Word by. Linda Trice

The Three Bears by. Paul Galdone

Sweet Potato Pie by. Kathleen D. Lindsey

Grandma's Records by. Eric Velasquez

Stompin At The Savoy by. Bebe Moore Campbell

Karate Hour by. Carol Nevius

Tonio's Cat by. Mary Calhoun

Fox On The Job by. James Marshall

Arthur And The School Pet by. Marc Brown

Jamaica And Brianna by. Juanita Havill

Arthur's Pet Business by. Marc Brown

From Cocoa Beans To Chocolate by. Robin Nelson

Dale Robinson

Sense Pass King—"A Story From Cameroon" by. Kartrin Tchana

Up Up Up It's Apple Picking Time by. Jody Fickes Shapiro

Jimi Sounds Like A Rainbow—A Story Of The Young Jimi Hendrix by. Gary Golio

God Gave Us You by. Lisa Tawn Bergren

John Brown—His Fight For Freedom by. John Hendrix

For The Love Of Soccer by. Pele

Just As Good—"How Larry Doby Changed America's Game" by. Chris Crowe

Muhammad Ali—"The People's Champion" by. Walter Dean Myers

A Picture Book of Harry Houdini (picture book biography) by.
David A. Alder
Michael S. Alder &
Matt Collins

Playing To Win: The Story of Althea Gibson by. Karen Deans & Elbrite Brown

Tiki & Ronde Barber—"Teammates" by. Tiki & Ronde Barber

Carter G. Woodson by. Patricia & Fredrick McKissack

Tiki & Ronde Barber—"By My Brothers Side" by. Tiki & Ronde Barber

Muhammad Ali: The People's Champion by. Karen Deans & Alix Delinois

My Uncle Martin's—"Big Heart" by. Angela Farris Watkins, Phd.

The Champ: The Story of Muhammad Ali by. Tonya Bolden

Tiki & Ronde Barber—"Game Day" by. Tiki & Ronde Berber

Dale Robinson

Monsieur Marceau by. Leda Schubert

Kenya's Song by Linda Trice

Spirit Seeker—John Coltrane's Musical Journey by. Gary Golio

The Honeybee Man by. Lela Nargi & Kyrsten Brooker

Ron's Big Mission by. Rose Blue & Corinne J. Naden

The Real McCoy—The Life of An African American Inventor by. Wendy Towle

The Story of Ruby Bridges by. Robert Coles

I, Matthew Henson by. Carole Boston Weatherford

Craft Artist

Glass Artists I've Met

Harvey Littleton—Met & Response to Letter

Judith Schaechter—Met & Response to Letter

Dante Marioni—Met

Susan Taylor Glasgow—Met & Response to Letter

Therman Statom—Met & Response to Letter through Mary Ann "toots" Zynsky

Mary Ann "toots" Zynsky—Response to Letter

Lino Tagliapietra—Met, Book & Autograph

Dale Chihuly—No Response to Letter

Alan Goldfarb—Met 4 times, Response to Letter & received a Glass Bowl and Cup

William Morris—No Response to my Letter, Book

Timothy Tate—Met twice

Mary Shaffer—Met & She was very "Nasty"

Dale Robinson

Howard Ben Tre—Response to Letter

Dan Dailey—Met & Book

Linda MacNeil—Met & Book

Josh Simpson—Met twice & Purchase his DVD

Paul Stankard—Met

Cappy Thompson—Response to Letter

Jon Kuhn—No Response to Letter but sent me a Book of his art

Sidney Hutter—Met & Autograph

Ricky Bernstein—Response to Letter

Gary Genetti—Met & Response to Letter

Carrie Gustafson—Met

Peter Secrest-Met

Wood Artists I've Met

Kim Schmahmann—Met 3 Times & Response to Letter

John Cederquist—Met twice & Response to Letter

Michelle Holzapfel—Met twice

Mark Lindquist—Met & Response to Letter

Christian Burchard—Met & Response to Letter

Mark Sfirri—Met

Sam Maloof-Autograph

Jay Rogers—Met twice & Response to Letter

Peter M. Petrochko—Met & Response to Letter

William Hunter—Response to Letter

Wendell Castle—Met & No Response to Letter

Jacob Cress—Met twice & Response to Letter (Oops! Chair)

Ron Kent—Response to Letter

Michael D. Mode—Met

Jay Whyte—Met

Judy Rand—Met

Dale Robinson

Fiber Artists I've Met

Virginia R. Harris—Response to Letter

Arline Fisch—Response to Letter

Tammie Bowser—Met

Carolyn Mazloomi—Response to Letter

Francia Patti—Met

Samantha Hodge-Williams—Met

Mary A. Jackson—Met twice

Ceramic Artists I've Met

Debra W. Fritts—Met & Response to Letter

Mariko Swisher—Met & Response to Letter

Henry Cavanagh—Response to Letter

Connie Kiener—Met & response to Letter

Dale Robinson

Paper Artists I've Met

Holly Anne Mitchell—Met & Response to Letter (Cathy Comics)

Akiko Sugiyama—Met twice, Response to Letter & Received Art Work

Jasmine

Jasmine 2.0

Master of the Puzzle

The world's greatest puzzler
is my little girl
Who pieced them all together
while she sits on the floor

It could be one hundred pieces
or five hundred in the box
she'll take the time to finish
under two days

She started when she was six
I thought she would stop
but she was so determined
to get that puzzle done

Matches all the colors
works from the outside in
no matter how complicated
she finishes them in the end

Dale Robinson

Time to Read a Book

Let's read a book
before you go to bed
fun dreams of love
dance inside your head

Sometimes we read one
other times we read more
it's the happy times together
that makes life fun

As we go to the library
to turn in our books
seeing your beautiful smile
when you pick up new books

Then go home and read them
one book at a time
then say our prayers
until tomorrow comes

Off To Nursery School

Let's go get you registered
in your favorite nursery school
so all the world can see
how wonderful you are

You'll learn about the ABCs
then count the 123s
afternoons go outside
to feel the playground breeze

Interact with the other kids
brings the best out of you
then go home to Mom and Dad
when your day is through

Showing them the things you learning
all the friends you made
iron out your clothes tonight
to go to school next day

Jassy The Great

Time to play some basketball
my little Jassy girl
one day you'll grow up
to be the best in the world

Time to play some softball
my little Jassy girl
one day you'll grow up
to be the best in the world

Then we'll play golf
you'll be the next superstar
shoot in the mid sixties
to win golfing titles

Dad let's go play soccer
then we'll play lacrosse
teach me everything
so I can be the best

Jasmine

She came into the world
weighing only a pound
don't let her die God
want to show her around

We'll pray on our knees
before we go to sleep
to make her body strong
until she comes home

She'll have teddy bears
to play with at home
teach her ballet
to dance to at home

Guess it's all true
it's all in God's hands
for our beautiful girl
who was born in this world

Cutting Of The Gut

Friday you were sick
Sunday got them out
thought you would die
instead of walking about

Sixty percent of gut
was taken out of you
the Nurses were so comforting
made us feel less blue

A bag was attached to her side
a Broviac in her chest
needs to get to four pounds
to reattach the rest

NEC was the culprit
all the food didn't digest
that's why she was sick
her intestines took a hit

Thank you God almighty
they got to her in time
if it wasn't for your touch
we're both out of our minds

Chips

Dad I want the orange chips!
Here my Jazzy girl
Try not to get the barbeque
All over the chair

Mom I want the green chips
I don't see why not
Try not to eat the chips
While you sleep in the bed

Now I want the red chip
Not until after dinner
You won't have any for camp
If you eat them all

Trail mix please!!!
Saving that for tomorrow
When you come home
From a hard day at camp

Rice Eating Girl

Shrimp fried rice
or just plain rice
doesn't matter to her
as long as it's rice

She'll eat some chicken
will eat the lamb
but there must be rice
sitting on her plate

Ever Sunday night
she has rice and beans
along with curry goat
and a cold drink to drink

So if you see a girl
eating a bowl of rice
it's my jazzy girl
eating plates of rice

Frozen Ice Cream

One scoop for you
one scoop for me
driving in the car
for some ice cream

Sometimes I'll get a pint
other times a sugar cone
so many flavors
that I can't decide

My favorite is French Vanilla
praline and cream for my wife
Jasmine doesn't really care
as long as its ice cream

No matter if it's summer
or the dead of winter
can't go without the taste
of some delicious ice cream

Daddy (Dale)

Remember me sweetheart
when no longer around
if you're sad and lonely
just read my poems

My love for you
goes deeper than my words
so dry your tears
I'm always there

To bring back memories
of things we did
so dry your tears
I'm always there

Read to you each night
before you went to sleep
played catch with the ball
after you ate

Walked with you to camp
we went to the park
my love for you
is always around

Aftercare

From the time she was six
she went to aftercare
the bus dropped her off
at the end of the day

Involved in activities
making arts and crafts
playing with other children
she's having a blast

A kind woman helps her
become more independent
slowly letting her go
don't want her dependent

When she becomes thirteen
she can no longer go
have to find another place
while I work during the day

Impression Girl

As she runs to the door
to greet me from work
she gives me love
that quenches my thirst

As we dance together
to our favorite tunes
I feel as happy
as the man in the moon

The real world is having
a child in your life
to care for each day
and tuck in at night

Who loves you when things
are bad in your life
that gives you the reason
to go on and fight

Hair Cut

Have a head of hair
or no hair at all
no matter to me
you're still my jassy girl

Had your first haircut
at the age of twelve
no more cutting
your hair to hell

To me you're better
with shorter hair
it just fits your face
you're an attractive girl.

Love you just as you are
no matter the size
of the hair you possess
on the top of your head

Love Force

Beauty is a human being
who loves the world around
smells a fragrant flower
that grows from out the ground

Beauty is humanity
who can smile at the world
when things in it go wrong
his faith in God provides

Love is such a precious thing
when you hold it in your arms
imagine if the world can see
the beauty love can show

Love is all around you
you need to look around
share it with a little child
even for a while

The Story Of Fried Chicken

Her eyes pop out
when she sees chicken legs
she tries to grab one
without any delay

Runs around the house
with that leg in her hand
drawing attention
while she ran

Then she'll stop
to hold it in the air
try taking it away
if you dare

She'll scream and bawl
till you give it back
then pick another
right off the stack

Just a little thing
so happy and proud
proclaiming her life
with a voice so loud

Who's The Prettiest Girl

Who's the prettiest girl in town
Jasmine! Jasmine!
Who's the prettiest girl in town
Jasmine! Jasmine!

Who's the prettiest girl in town
her name is Jassy girl

She's so sweet
her love can't be beat
I want to take her home
to kiss her tiny feet

Who's the prettiest girl in town
Jasmine! Jasmine!
Who's the prettiest girl in town
Jasmine! Jasmine!

Who's the prettiest girl in town
her name is Jassy girl

Follow the Bouncing Ball

Bounce around the house
bounce around the park
catch the ball from out the sky
bounce around some more

Playing catch with you
roll it back to you
so much joy enjoying life
as we bounce the ball

Family life's the only thing
that's safe from the world
have the memory deep inside
when we play with the ball

Bounce it high in the air
or kick it across the yard
the joy of life's not money
but playing catch with my girl

Jump Rope Skipping

Jump skip one
jump skip two
playing with your jump rope
until the evening comes

Skip the rope three times
now you're up to eight
girl! you keep going
until you get it right

Mom and I turn the rope
while you spin around
keep on going sweetheart
one day you'll master it

Part of one memory
I've shared with you all
the joy of your childhood
lived all over again

Scooter

Riding up and down
pushing for more speed
free as the wind
around the trees

Even when I put a chair
in the middle driveway
she'll just go around
to the back of the yard

Can remember a time
when she ran round
now it's the scooter
in the backyard

Rides it as if
she rode it before
my little girl is growing
before my eyes

Playground Beyond

Jasmine 2.0 (Playground Beyond)

The Circus Electric Dreamer

I'm the ring master
of this circus electric dream
will introduce a show
that is hard to believe

There are acrobatic wordsmiths
using death defying lines
muscle bound strong wills
lifting profound minds

Contortion twisted mind thinks
who invent Vocabulary
to astonish all the people
that sit in the crowd

Psychic clown mind trips
spray the crowd with whimsical
to experience all the fun
their minds try to hide

Now the animals of confusion
are getting out of their chairs
to face all the perils

of this death defying world

Dale Robinson

The Cosmic Beyonds

Heard celestial Guitars
beyond the clouds
funky finger Bass thumps
are along for the ride

Enlightened air Flutes
floating through space
Keyboards of the outer world
keep up with the pace

That big bad Drum blast
puts them all together
now they're ready
to take the show on the road

You'll hear this band
in a galaxy near you
tickets are on sale
at the galactic plane

The name of the band
is the Cosmic Beyonds
taken from the pages
of a gifted mind

A Bar Of Chocolate

I'm a chocolate nougat candy bar
sweet taste deep down your soul
whipped up to smooth consistency
that defies confining space

I'm not your common flavor
you see from week to week
or that new taste sensation
that you'll never taste again

Just covered in chocolate
with the caramel in between
a credit to my race of skin
to taste this nice to you

Wrapped in red cellophane
ready to be consumed
nothings truly better
than to take a bite of me

Dale Robinson

Surfer

Been a fantastic ride
enjoyed every moment
always endless fun
now to get it done

Surf the tide of thought waves
out shoot the curl
steady on my wordplay
until the waves die down

Waiting on the beach
were memories of my dreams
telling me to go out
and catch the big dream

Caught the big one
filled my head with ideas
trying to ride it out
till the words begin to sing

A surfing world record
dance across the page
receive congratulations
on the world stage

Adventures Of Princess Teddy Bear

Goodnight princess teddy bear
your eyes are fast asleep
wake to morning's gold delights
let's go for Ice Cream

Snuggle up between my arms
your soul is close to me
dream of elephant circus parades
subconscious dream away

Deep inside the conscious pool
are dreams of what you felt
reality merge within your mind
the point of being real

Wake up my lovely teddy bear
let's fly through candy corn
across the rainbow chocolate sky
where playground children roam

In The Land Of Bling

Poor Mister bling bling
has lost his dream
of seeing his name
on the silver screen

Poor Miss bling bling
had a Diamond ring
found out it was fake
then she started to scream

Kids now have icy bling
around their necks
too bad their minds are filled
with gangsta dreams

That's how it goes
in the land of bling
possessions are more important
than the human being

There's One In Every Pack (Cards)

I'm the Joker in the pack
that hasn't been unwrapped
the craze one of fifty three
that hasn't been figured out

And though one of fifty three
without a number count
wild next to any card
to increase the impact

I'm no ordinary diamond
not the heart of your dreams
didn't have a club date
never held any spades

But I was the only one
who simply broke the mold
never been confined
by any form of rules

In The Hourglass Sand Absurd

O hand of the shifting sand
that slide through fingers grasp
what happens in oblivion
left to the power be

Afraid you should not
ticket of the one way life
your fun has just begun
when the world's not after you

Think you seen it all
intelligent beyond the grasp
education of no account
are left without a clue

Onward tiny grain sands
life encountering everyday's
a mouth left wide open
with really nothing to say

Amusement Park Day Dream

Mind has become an amusement park
entertainment for the mind
can be silly as I want to be
expression makes me free

Can say what I want to say
without barriers to my thoughts
deep inside my memory pool
the silliness comes out

Comes out in every imaginable way
fun that delights the crowd
stretching out to new frontiers
a craft develop thru years

A silly man of fun
who enjoys amusing himself
gone beyond the spoken word
to an imaginary word of my own

The Strength Of My (Wife)

Lovely beauty wife of mine
who brings joy to my life
love you with my heart and soul
your kiss send me to moon

That's why I'm thankful for your love
you always have my ears
to listen to your problems
that smash your glow of joy

You are the flower in my life
forever is my love
strength that moves the mountain
that somehow get in my way

Love is just a fleeting thing
will always hold it tight
never let it get away
because of any neglect

Whipping Up A Dish

Pinch of imagination
dash of surreal dreams
mixed in a cup of words
to create a poetic scene

Baked in an oven
at three hundred degrees
in the next two hours
will see how it be

Taken out the oven
nice crust of verbs
isn't it wonderful
eating these tasty words

The real test comes
when the world has a taste
if they ask for seconds
my dish was a success

Relaxation

I'm the marshmallow pulled apart
you see inside within
I'm the jigsaw puzzle figured out
if you take the time

The method of my madness
is just having fun
if this is not your way
then you need to take the time

Too much fear and sadness
that drains the soul of life
time to take the flight escape
to paradise mind relax

You cannot live in tight restraint
one day you're blow apart
and land in some asylum
to die in lonely blight

Is It Reality Or Is It Just Me

Upside down in the land of nod
fools live in idle dreams
too much power
too much greed
your judgment seeds have bled

Too much sleep inside your eyes
for you to count the sheep
a Sun has fell from out the sky
to burn your naked feet

I'm laughing to the point of tears
a standing wall is near
to catch me from your accusations
thrown to ease your fears

Ease your mind and have some fun
before you leave the plane
so play the game with much delight
before your final flight

A Cosmic Soul Brothers Adventure

Just a cosmic soul brother
throwing tidbits to the world
the impact of my words
shine bright as the golden sun

No antichrist superstar
proclaiming he's the one
gave my thanks and praise
to the one who lives above

Why such a problem
when I talk this way to you
was it because my thinking
was not of this world

Must educate the ignorant
who deal in deadly games
showing them an example
on how to truly behave

Hello to all the people
who are into spiritual plans
one day we'll be together
in the beautiful new lands

Until we meet again
I say goodbye to you
when my eyes reopen
a world abound in love

Wordplay Olympics

The Olympics of wordplay
is here at last
who will win gold
in the poetry class

There's the Slam Poets
practicing their craft
over there the Haiku's
battle for the dream

I'm in the Surreal category
battling subconscious minds
waiting for my turn
as I stand in line

Hundreds of different styles
battle for gold
now the games have started
let the words flow

Didn't win this year
but boy! I had fun
shaking hands with everyone
all came as one

Brothers in arms
as we walked out the door
next time my words
will put you on the floor

The Funny Page

Cartoons were required reading
once as a child
fueled my imagination
to where I am now

Taught me how to be
anything that I want
no limits to my imagination
left alone to be free

Parents were my encouragement
always smile when passing by
they were like amusement parks
letting me enjoy the rides

All of this is paying off
in the form of this book
you laugh and smile on the floor
when you take a look

Hot As A Baby Back Rib

Feel like a Barbeque
baked in the sun
please God Almighty
would you turn off the sun

Just like a baby back
grilled golden brown
good for consumption
but not walking around

Spread the barbeque sauce
but not too thick!
don't want to burn
to a total crisp

This is how it's like
to cook in the sun
there are other ways inside
for you to have fun

Unsolve Problem Solvers

To the question mark enigmas
walking around today
when will you stop
watching talk show host

Wanderer of the what happen
figure out you try
solutions are in from of vou
if only you take advice‘

Brain teasing Analyst
on the verge of breakdown
you can make this easy
instead of struggle mess

This is no concept
applications are at the front
easy to figure out
without mouthpiece advice

Out Of The Blue Philosophy

Tick Tock the mind of space
the seconds march in time
every precious moments of life
are measured carefully

People in your life and times
gather to share your dreams
thanking God high above
for blessings you receive

Love has matter all the time
time wasting not to be
freedom's just a state of mind
when you know the key

How you look at life you see
when things are falling free
future facing is no fear
to people who are dear

Inspired From Above

Think Arts not God inspiring
put down that Art
get out of your chair
just simply walk away

God made the brain
for you to create
don't want to ever hear
you make that mistake

He gave you the power
to write down these lines
if that's not awe inspiring
I think you lost your mind

Before you make anything
just look high above
and count all of your blessings
for the talent you have

Jasmine's Bio

Jasmine 2.0 (Jasmine Bio)

Jasmine was a Brownie Girl Scout

From 7 to 8 years old.

Jasmine was a Junior Girl Scout

From 9 to 11 years old.

Jasmine listens to WGTS 91.9 on the Radio.

She enjoys the Christian Artists

on the Radio Station.

Jasmine's Favorite Activities

Puzzles

Going to Church

Catching Balls

Scooters

Jump Ropes

Reading Books to her

Kicking Balls in the Backyard

Roller skating

My Wife and I got Jasmine a Karaoke Machine

on Christmas 2010

"She never puts it down."

Mom (Christa), Dad (Dale) and Jasmine would go to

Baskin Robbins every other month

to get Ice Cream

When Jasmine went to Springhill Lake Elementary

School from six to twelve years old.

It was one of the happiest times in my life.

When Jasmine was six, I (Daddy) would take her

to the playground to play.

Jasmine and I (Dad) would go to the Public Library to get

Books to read with my library Card.

Sometimes after going to the Library, we would go to

Prince George's Plaza

to get Cinnamon Sugar Pretzels at Auntie Anne's.

At the age of nine in 2003, Jasmine

went to the Circus for the first time.

At the age of ten in 2004, Jasmine

went to the Universal Soul Circus.

Jasmine went to Buck Lodge Middle School

from age 12 to 14 years of age.

One of my fondness memories

was taking Jasmine to camp at M-NCPPC Rollingcrest

Community Center on my (2) days off from work.

Jasmine has been in the M-NCPPC

Traveling Teens Greenbelt Camp

since the age of fourteen.

Jasmine was born July *29,* 1994 on Friday at 11:31AM.

She weighed 1lb. 5ozs. at birth at Holy Cross Hospital.

Jasmine loves riding her scooter.

Activities Jasmine Loves

Activities Jasmine Loves

Loves eating Cinnamon Sugar Pretzels at Auntie Anne's

Loves going to Church every Sabbath

Loves for me to read to her my Bible Cards

Loves listening to Religious Music on WPGA 91.9

Loves playing with Puzzles

Loves going to the Library

Loves going on Field Trips at School

Loves eating Ice Cream in Cones or in Cups

Loves going to the Movies and eating Popcorn

Loves going to M-NCPPC Traveling Teens Greenbelt Camp

Lo0ves coloring with Crayons and Color Pens

Loves eating Rice (Shrimp Fried, Chicken Fried or Plain Rice)

Loves eating Pizzas—Ground Beef

Loves eating Pancakes or Waffles

Dad (Dale) & Mom (Christa) took Jasmine

To Luray Caverns in June 2009.

"She calls them Luray Caves."

Jasmine loves Catching and Kicking the ball

in the Backyard.

Jasmine went to Frances Fuchs Developmental Center

until she was six years old.

Jasmine loves any kind of Rice

(Fried, Plain, Shrimp or Chicken).

Jasmine loves any kind of Potato Chips

(Barbeque, Cheese, Green Onion, Ranch).

I, Dad (Dale) would spend one hour with Jasmine

at Northwestern High School working on her

Reading and Counting.

In 1995, the first solid food Jasmine ate was

Ice Cream (Vanilla).

Jasmine went to Amish Country

In Pennsylvania in the summer of 1998.

Christa, Jasmine & Me

would go to the movies.

and eat a big box of popcorn.

Jasmine loves going to church.

Activities Jasmine and Me (Dale) Love To Do Together

Eating Cinnamon Sugar Pretzels

Going to the Library

Reading Books Together

Going to the Movies

Looking at DVD (Movies) Together

Looking at Television Together

Me and Mom (Christa) taking her to Luray Caverns

Me and Mom (Christa) taking her to Restaurants

Dad's Bio

Jasmine 2.0 (Dad's Bio) Dale's

Started going to an Adventist Church

On Saturday March 7, 1987.

"Never went back to a Sunday Church."

Started working for the Smithsonian Institution

on October 31, 1988.

"After Twenty-Five years, I'm truly thankful

that I still have a job."

Stop watching network Television since 1977.

Christa, my wife, was born on March 8, 1955

in Jamaica.

Started writing my first poem on January 30, 1985.

Shaved for the first time on June 1973.

Went to Karate Class at June Rhee in 1973 at Fifteen.

"Nobody Bothers Me."

Got a Transistor Radio on my eighteenth birthday

July 7, 1966.

Was born on July 7, 1958 on Monday at 4:35 A.M.

Met my wife, Christa, for the first time

on September 21, 1984.

At the age six, I ran from Bees on a wet pool

deck at camp.

Punishment: Had to sit by the Lifeguards chair

for three weeks.

Left my camp group hike at age eleven

Wanted to explore on my own

"It took the whole camp two hours to find me."

Punishment: The Whole Camp didn't
talk to me for two weeks.

"I acted as though everything was normal."

It was only when they talk to me that I DIDN'T
UNDERSTAND WHY THEY WERE MAD AT ME!

They forgave me because I look innocent in their eyes
and truly didn't understand why they were mad.

Saw both Tron Movies

"Tron"—1982

"Tron Legacy"—2010

Favorite Jamaican Dishes

Jerk Pork

Jerk Chicken.

Ox—Tails

Gout Meat

Ackee & Saltfish

Graduated from Archbishop Carroll High School

on June 2, 1977.

Saw the Movie "Star Wars" two weeks after

Graduating from high School on June 19, 1977.

Married my Wife on January 5, 1985

"Even though we have our ups and downs

It's been a wonderful twenty-eight years."

Activities My Wife (Christa) Loves

Listening to Oldies Records

Looking at Old Movies

Love Having Family and Friends Around

Loves Jewelry (Necklaces, Bracelets, Earrings & Watches)

Love going to Concerts

Loves going to Theatrical Plays

Loves Traveling to Different Places

Only one in my Family born on an odd day

Dad—November 16

Mom—April 26

Mark—December 4

Lynn—January 22

Me (Dale)—July 7 ****

Was part of the swimming team for two years.

"They were known as the *Stafford Sea Devils*"

"Takoma Park Swin Club"

From 1971-1973

Met a Girl named Cynthia Pree who broke

my heart because she had a Boy friend

She was born March 23, 1961.

Had my first crush on a Capricorn girl name

Lauren Graham born on December 26, 1958.

This was in 1971.

Had my second crush on a red bone Gemini girl name

Shari Jennifer born on May 30, 1959.

This was in 1972.

Favorite Restaurants

Sizzler's—No Longer in Existence

Bob's Big Boy—No Longer in Existence

Olive Garden

Outback Steakhouse

Bennigan's (happy, happy, happy birthday)—
No Longer in Existence

IHOP—International House of Pancakes

Worked at my first job at Riggs Bank

on December 7, 1981.

Both of My Brothers finished College

Mark—University of Pennsylvania

Bachelor's Degree (BS) Biology

Lynn—University of Pennsylvania

Bachelor's Degree (BS) Business Administration
With a Minor in Economics

Dale Fisher Robinson

Born July 7, 1958 at 4:35 A.M.

Sun—Cancer in 1st House

Moon—Pisces in 10th House

Mercury—Leo in 2nd House

Venus—Gemini in 12th House

Mars—Aries in? House

Jupiter—Libra in 4th House

Saturn—Sagittarius in 6th House

Uranus—Leo in 3rd House

Neptune—Scorpio in 5th House

Pluto—Virgo in 3rd House

After getting this chart done in 1983, I threw all of my Astrology book in the Garbage Can.

God is the only way to salvation, not in the stars above.

African Continent

Jasmine 2.0 (African Continent)

Tunisia

Capitol—Tunis

Colonial Power—France
Independence—March 20, 1956
Natural Resources—lead, zinc, salt, iron ore, petroleum phosphates

Djibouti

Capitol—Djibouti

Colonial Power—France
Independence—June 27, 1977
Natural Resources—gold, clay, granite, limestone marble, salt,
                        diatomic, gypsum pumice, petroleum,
                        geothermal areas

Benin

Capitol—Porto Novo

Colonial Power—France
Independence—August 1, 1960
Natural Resources—limestone, marble, timber, petroleum small off
        shore oil deposits, hydropower

Botswana

Capitol—Gaborone

Colonial Power—England
Independence—Sept. 30, 1966
Natural Resources—diamonds, copper, nickel, salt soda ash,
        potash, coal, iron ore silver

Togo

Capitol—Lome

Colonial Power—France
Independence—April 27, 1960
Natural Resources—limestone, marble, phosphates arable land

Lesotho

Capitol—Maseru

Colonial Power—England
Independence—Oct. 4, 1966
Natural Resources—water, sand, clay, building stone diamonds,
                            agricultural & grazing lands

Madagascar

Capitol—Antananarivo

Colonial Power—France
Independence—June 26, 1960
Natural Resources—graphite, chromium, coal, bauxite salt, quartz,
                tar, sands, mica, fish semi precious stones,
                hydropower

Gabon

Capitol—Libreville

Colonial Power—France
Independence—August 17, 1960
Natural Resources—petroleum, natural gas, diamonds niobium,
                manganese, uranium, gold timber, iron ore,
                hydropower

Chad

Capitol—N'Djamena

Colonial Power—France
Independence—August 11, 1960
Natural Resources—petroleum, uranium, neutrons, kaolin fish,
gold, limestone, sand & gravel, salt

Sudan

Capitol—Khartoum

Colonial Power—England
Independence—Jan. 1, 1956
Natural Resources—copper, zinc, tungsten, mica, silver gold,
petroleum, iron ore, chromium ore

Senegal

Capitol—Dakar

Colonial Power—France
Independence—August 20, 1960
Natural Resources—fish, phosphates, iron ore, gold copper,
titanium, peat

Mali

Capitol—Bamako

Colonial Power—France
Independence—Sept. 22, 1960
Natural Resources—gold, salt, kaolin, phosphates limestone,
uranium, gypsum, granite bauxite, iron
ore, tin, manganese, copper, petroleum,
hydropower

Algeria

Capitol—Algeria

Colonial Power—France
Independence—July 5, 1962
Natural Resources—petroleum, natural gas, iron ore, phosphates,
            uranium, lead, zinc

Ghana

Capitol—Accra

Colonial Power—England
Independence—March 6, 1957
Natural Resources—gold, timber, industrial diamonds bauxite,
            manganese, fish, rubber silver, hydropower,
            petroleum

Angola

Capítol—Luanda

Colonial Power—Portugal
Independence—Nov. 11, 1975
Natural Resources—petroleum, diamonds, iron ore, phosphates,
copper, feldspar, gold, bauxite, uranium

Uganda

Capitol—Kampala

Colonial Power—England
Independence—Oct. 9, 1962
Natural Resources—copper, cobalt, salt, limestone hydropower,
arable land, tin beryl, bismuth

Democratic Republic of The Congo

Capitol—Kinshasa

Colonial Power—Belgium
Independence—June 30, 1960
Natural Resources—diamonds, gold, copper, coltan, cobalt

Republic of The Congo

Capitol—Brazzaville

Colonial Power—France
Independence—Aug. 15, 1960
Natural Resources—petroleum, zinc, copper, uranium gold,
                  magnesium, lead, timber potash, natural gas,
                  phosphates

Central Africa Republic

Capitol—Bangui

Colonial Power—France
Independence—August 13, 1960
Natural Resources—diamonds, uranium, timber, gold oil,
hydropower.

Burkina Faso

Capitol—Ouagadougou

Colonial Power—France
Independence—Aug. 5, 1960
Natural Resources—manganese, limestone, marble gold (small
deposits), phosphates pumice, salt

Mozambique

Capitol—Maputo

Colonial Power—Portugal
Independence—June 25, 1975
Natural Resources—coal, titanium, natural gas, tantalum graphite,
hydropower

Zambia

Capitol—Lusaka

Colonial Power—England
Independence—Oct. 24, 1964
Natural Resources—copper, cobalt, zinc, lead, coal emeralds, gold,
silver, uranium hydropower

Sierra Leone

Capitol—Freetown

Colonial Power—England
Independence—Apr. 27, 1961
Natural Resources—diamonds, titanium ore, bauxite gold, iron ore,
petroleum, chromite petroleum hydropower

Zimbabwe

Capitol—Harare

Colonial Power—England
Independence—proclaimed—Nov. 11, 1965
recognized—Apr. 18, 1980
Natural Resources—coal, chromium ore, asbestos, gold nickel,
copper, iron ore, vanadium lithium, tin,
platinum

Swaziland

Capitol—Mbabane (Administrative)
       Lobamba (Royal & legislative)

Colonial Power—England
Independence—Sept. 6, 1968
Natural Resources—asbestos, coal, clay, tin ore, forests
                 hydropower, quarry, small gold and diamond
                 deposits

Equatorial Guinea

Capitol—Malabo

Colonial Power—Spain
Independence—Oct. 12, 1968
Natural Resources—petroleum, natural gas, timber, gold bauxite,
                 diamonds, tantalum sand & gravel, clay

Dale Robinson

Libya

Capitol—Tripoli

Colonial Powers—Italy, France, England
Independence—Italy—Feb. 10, 1947
France & England—Dec. 24, 1951
under united nations trusteeship

Natural Resources—petroleum, natural gas, gypsum

Egypt

Capitol—Cairo

Colonial Power—England
Independence—Feb. 28, 1922
Republic declared—June 18, 1953
National Day—July 23, 1952
Natural Resources—petroleum, natural gas, iron ore, talc
phosphates, manganese, limestone, lead, zinc,
gypsum, asbestos

Burundi

Capitol—Bujumbura

Colonial Power—Belgium
Independence—July 1, 1962
Natural Resources—nickel, uranium, cobalt copper, platinum, peat
vanadium, rare earth oxides

Namibia

Capitol Windhoek

Colonial Power—South Africa
Independence—March 21, 1990
Natural Resources—diamonds, copper, uranium, gold lead, tin,
lithium, salt, zinc, cadmium vanadium, natural
gas

Somalia

Capitol—Mogadishu

Colonial Powers—England and Italy
Independence—England—June 26, 1960
            Italy—July 1, 1960
Natural Resources—uranium, iron ore, tin, gypsum Bauxite,
            copper, salt

Morocco

Capitol—Rabat

Colonial Powers—France and Spain
Independence—France—March 2, 1956
            Spain—April 7, 1956
Natural Resources—phosphates, Iron ore, lead, zinc, fish salt,
            manganese, petroleum, hydropower

Eritrea

Capitol—Asmara

Independence—Ethiopia—May 24, 1993
Natural Resources—gold, copper, oil (possibly), zinc, potash, salt,
       fish, natural gas

Ethiopia

Capitol—Addis Ababa

Colonial Power—Italy
Independence—Abyssinia—1137
        partially occupied by Italy 1936-1941
        Democratic Republic—1991
Natural Resources—small reserves of gold, platinum, copper
       potash, natural gas, hydropower

Liberia

Capitol—Monrovia

Colonial Power—United States
Independence—July 26, 1847
ASC colonies consolidation—1821-1842

American Colonization Society
Formation by. African Americans
Natural Resources—iron ore, timber, gold, diamonds hydropower

Gambia

Capitol—Banjul

Colonial Power—England
Independence—Feb. 18, 1965
Republic Declared—Apr. 24, 1970
Natural Resources—tin, silica sand, zircon, clay, fish Titanium,
                              petroleum

Malawi

Capitol—Lilongwe

Colonial Power—England
Independence—July 6, 1964
Natural Resources—limestone, uranium, coal, bauxite hydropower,
          arable land

Niger

Capitol—Niamey

Colonial Power—France
Independence—declared—August 3, 1960
Natural Resources—uranium, coal, tin, iron ore, gold gypsum, salt,
          petroleum, phosphates molybdenum

Dale Robinson

Cote d' Ivoire

Capitol—Yamoussoukro

Colonial power—France
Independence—August 7, 1960
Natural Resources—rubber, petroleum, cocoa, plastics resin, coffee

Mauritania

Capitol—Nouakchott

Colonial Power—France
Independence—Nov. 28, 1960
Natural Resources—iron ore, gypsum, copper, phosphates
                 diamonds, gold, oil, fish

Rwanda

Capitol—Kigali

Colonial Power—Belgium
Independence—July 1, 1962
Natural Resources—gold, tin ore, tungsten ore, methane
     Hydropower, arable land

Guinea

Capitol—Conakry

Colonial Power—France
Independence—Oct. 2, 1958
Natural Resources—bauxite, iron ore, gold, diamonds uranium,
     fish, salt, hydropower

Tanzania

Capitol—Dodoma

Colonial Power—England
Independence—Tanganyika—Dec. 9, 1961
    Zanzibar—Jan. 12, 1964
    Merger—Apr. 26, 1964
Natural Resources—gold, nickel, tin, coal, iron ore, diamonds,
    gemstones, hydropower, natural gas,
    phosphates

Kenya

Capitol—Nairobi

Colonial Power—England
Independence—Dec. 12, 1963
Republic Declared—Dec. 12, 1964
Natural Resources—limestone, salt, soda ash, fluorspar, zinc,
    diatomite, gypsum, wildlife gemstones,
    hydropower

Cameroon

Capitol—Yaounde

Colonial Powers—France, England
Independence—France—Jan. 1, 1960
England—Oct. 1, 1961
Natural Resources—petroleum, bauxite, timber, iron ore
hydropower

Guinea-Bissau

Capitol—Bissau

Colonial Power—Portugal
Independence—declared—Sept. 24, 1973
recognized—Sept. 10, 1974
Natural Resources—fish, timber, phosphates, bauxite Clay, granite,
limestone, petroleum

Nigeria

Capitol—Abuja

Colonial Power—England
Independence—1914
Recognized/declared—Oct. 1, 1960
Republic/declared—Oct. 1, 1963
Natural Resources—petroleum, tin, lead, zinc niobium, iron ore,
                limestone natural gas, arable land

Mauritius

Capitol—Port Louis

Colonial Power—England
Independence—March 12, 1968
Republic—March 12, 1992
Natural Resources—arable land, fish

The Republic of South Sudan

Capitol—Juba

Independence—Sudan—July 9, 2011
Natural Resources—copper, zinc, tungsten, mica, silver, gold,
petroleum, iron ore, chromium ore

Western Sahara

Capitols—El Aaiun (Bir Moroccan)
Lehlou—temporary

Colonial Power—Spain
Independence—Nov. 14, 1975
Disputed sovereignty relinquished
Natural Resources—iron ore, phosphates

Seychelles

Capitol—Victoria

Colonial Power—England
Independence—July 29, 1976
Natural Resources—copra, cinnamon, vanilla, coconuts fish,
essential oils

Comoros

Capitol—Moroni

Colonial power—France
Independence—July 6, 1975

Sao Tome & Principe

Capitol—Sao Tome

Colonial Power—Portugal
Independence—July 12, 1975
Natural Resources—Cocoa

Cape Verde

Capitol—Praia

Colonial Power—Portugal
Independence—1975
Natural Resources—salt, fish

South Africa

Capitols—Pretoria (executive)
        Bloemfontein (judicial)
        Cape town (legislative)

Colonial Power—England
Independence—May 31, 1910
Statute of Westminster—Dec. 11, 1931
Apartheid—1948

Republic—May 31, 1961
        Left the British Commonwealth

Apartheid Ended—1990
Natural Resources—gem diamonds, platinum, gold salt, coal, iron
        ore, tin, nickel uranium, copper, manganese
        chromium, vanadium, phosphates antimony,
        natural gas

Racism 101

Jasmine 2.0 (Racism 101)

Gabby

She won Team Gold
won Gold in the Individual All Around
will her face be on the box
of some Corn Flakes

First African American women
to win the All Around
first American Gymnast
to win both Individual and Team Gold

Then black apologist for racism came out
talking about her black skin
because you wanted to fine fault
even thou she won All Around

Then the racist follow behind
agreeing to what they say
because you wanted the White Girl
to win the All Around

Then you talked about her hair
and about her uniform
not being in the colors
of the American Flag

But I loved her response
when confronted by this hate
you said! this is who I am!
not going to change for your convenience!

And the sportsmanship you displayed
when you lost Balance Beam
should be an example
for the rest of the girls on the team
When you lost Uneven Bars
you didn't make excuses
to you it was an off day
you would try to win next time

You're America's sweetheart
other Athlete's admired you
now Girls of all races
want to get involve in Gymnastic

with two Gold Metals
you can help your Sister and Mother
who believe in you from the beginning
that you could achieve greatness

Get some Lawyers who will protect you
when people try to take advantage
enjoy your fame Flying Squirrel
on your gymnastic world tour

Get some Accountants who'll protect your money
when people try to take advantage
things will change for you fast
after you enjoy your gymnastic tour

Susan Rice

So Big and Bad
going after Ms. Rice
because of what happen at our Embassy
by Terrorist in Libya

All because of a Viro Video
that was done in America
sent across the Internet
that inflame anger in the Muslim World

You didn't bother to go to the Briefings
that the CIA and FBI conducted
to get all of the facts
instead of attacking Ms. Rice

Ms. Rice doesn't make policy
her marching orders come from the President
so she was following orders
that came from the top

She was given a White House release
when she went on Television
if you had problems with what she said
then jump on the people who gave her that release

How dare you say
she must meet with you
so you can determine if she's qualified
for nomination for Secretary of State

Someone who graduated
almost at the bottom of his class
when he was a student
at the Naval Academy

Compared to someone
who was a Rhode Scholar
who was a tenured Professor
at a prestigious University in America

Because you were angry
when President Obama won reelection
you thought there was an opening
to discredit a presidential nominee

Trying to get your Republican Colleagues
to push for a Democrat from Massachusetts
so you can get an additional seat
in the Senate chambers

Ms. Rice is well qualified
for Secretary of State
even Hillary Clinton felt
she would be perfect for the job

Using Words Against You

An Agriculture Secretary
had to pull off the road
to text in her resignation
for some perceived racist remarks

Only to find out
that a producer at Fox
didn't like the NAACP
saying The Tea Party have racist elements

It was another Reverend Wrigh
over an hour long dinner speech
cut down to twenty-five minutes
to make a person appear racist

Can't get your racist thinking
to except we have a Black President
if you can't get the Black President
we'll go after the Black Congress

Now you charged Mister Rangels
then you go after Miss Waters
you can charged White Congress Members
with the same ethics charges

Dale Robinson

How To Handle Racial Profiling

Witness said it was suitcases
You said they were backpacks
Witness said you didn't take her statement
You said she made a statement

Sergeant Pinocchio of Cambridge
Your nose has grown long
Making yourself look good
By falsifying your report

A solution to racial profiling
Is to have a beer party
That never discusses the behavior
Of some racist cops

Fried Chicken on the table
With greasy hot fries
Sit down and forget
About your black pride

No need for you to worry
There's no racial profiling
No active participants
In this diverse group

To busy enjoying beers
To talk of police brutality
Now come on shake hands!
Bring this dispute to an end

While paranoid talk show hosts
Raise the flames of polarization
Putting the races at each other's throats
Because police won't admit their wrong

A politically expedient President
Who's afraid of police unions
Threatening not to suppose him
If he doesn't take their side

We're all one America
If we accept the white way of thinking
And called a bunch of racist
When they can't handle the truth

Thank you all for coming
To this reconciliation beer party
That helps me to focus away
From black discrimination

Public Radio Bigot # 1

Radio Bigot still resides
as a Radio Talk Show Host
doesn't have the decency to apologize
to a women he called a slut

But he represents millions of White Men
who exhibit these same attitudes
using racist epithets on Black People
while treating women as sex objects

When he lost over forty sponsors
he refer to them as French Fries
that dropped from the carton
onto a food tray

It's the root of the problem
they're losing some of their control
that they once had on Black People
as well as on Women

Then the ugliness comes out
when they are unhappy
so they resort to racist behavior
to make them feel superior

Few Republicans in both houses
denounced this Radio Talk Host
because they embraced his attitude
when it comes to Black's and Women

So he keeps on hiding
behind his First Amendment rights
it's time to tell this bigot
those rights fall also to his victims

If I Own Clear Channel
that aired his Radio Program
I'll cut off his microphone
tell him to peddle his garbage somewhere else

It's time people have civility
and have a sense of decency
so we can put these race baiters
in the garbage where they belong

Missy Arizona

You think you're so cute
pointing your finger in President Obama's face
when everybody thinks
you're acting like a fool

It's bad enough that black people
have to deal with racist stupidity
instead of a racist white women
who thinks she's telling a Black Man off

A Black Man who has achieved more
than what she achieved in life
who did an excellent job
cleaning up this Republican mess

The party that spend
like a bunch of drunken sailors
on a two day pass
from a tour of duty

Or that lady from Arizona
who passed an immigration bill
that gave the Police the license
to profile people of color

Ladies and Gentlemen
we present to you
A Black Man from the Ivy Leagues
who achieved great things

Over there Ladies and Gentlemen
are a bunch of White People
who cover up their stupidity
trying to make idiocy profound

Can we all get along
without hearing your brand of racism
that derived from your hatred
when a Black Man achieves power

Carforgetson

Brainwashed Black People
are coming out everyday
believing what White Society
said what America is all about

The greatness of America
that was denied to us
because our black skin wasn't as white
as the white people that owned us

Want to push their America Philosophy
on minorities in this country
and want people of color
to forget about the shame of their racist history

America the Beautiful
wasn't great in my eyes
when people of color
were treated less than animals

Black's were put in chains
on the continent of Africa
then boarded ships of slavery
on their way to America

Sold to rich White People
on Cotton and Tobacco Plantations
worked them till they died
from Sun up to Moon high

Didn't matter if they were Sugar
or any other type of Plantation
they worked Black People
for the profit of White Slave Owners

They were White Peoples Property
to do whatever they wanted
if Black's try to escape
they were shot dead while they ran

Had children by their White Wives
while having children with Black Slave Women
want proof that that happen
look at the third President of America

Who had a personal affair
with one of his Black Slave Women
Justice Tanner of The Supreme Court said
Black People had no rights recognized by the Constitution

Dale Robinson

If You Don't Win Like Tiger! Forget Notoriety!!

Win a Mickey Mouse tournament
in Charlotte North Carolina
you won't get the notoriety
unless you win like Tiger Woods

A different player from week to week
wins a different tournament
if they don't win like Tiger
no one really cares

It's just like Jordan in Basketball
or Gretzky in Hockey
if it's not spectacular like Tiger
forget about the television audience

If you don't win Major Championships
the way Tiger Woods does
people will still speak of Tiger
and tell the rest who are you

It's the reason Jack's a legend
and talk of the Big Three
it was known as a rivalry
because they beat each other

There are players who win tournaments
other players who win Majors
but then there's Tiger Woods
who's spotlight blocks everyone out

So all you Golf Announcers
and Ex Golf Players on Golf Shows
you may not like it
but that's the way it is

Some of them have won four or five tournament
others couldn't take the pressure
now they have become experts
on why Tiger should go back to Butch

With Butch he won Eight Majors
with Hank he won Six Majors
he gets a new Swing Coach
now they criticize the change

You guys should just shut up!
only one guy has more Majors
you don't see him criticize Tiger
on how he's playing his game

That's the real reason
why Golf Media people are so upset
they want to talk about other Golfers
but the audience wants them to speak of Tiger

It's always been that way
when a great player appears
Golfers step in the footprints of greatness
then you'll receive notoriety!!

Trying to Use Republican History to Scandalize A President

That Director of the IRS
who was checking Tea Party taxes
was appointed by George Bush
under a Republican administration

So Main Stream Republicans
thought Tea Party Republicans
were a bunch of crazy radicals
that needed to be checked on

No scandal under Obama
was ever found
those things were done
under a Republican administration

The Patriot Act was put in place
after September Eleven
during the Bush administration
under a Republican Control Congress

The Terrorist Surveillance Act
was put in place
during the Bush administration
under a Republican Control Congress

Anyone suspected of a Terrorist Act
can be charged under the Patriot Act
then thrown in jail
without due process in court

No Lawyer can defend you
no access to any court records
can be use to prove
that you didn't commit the crime

All under the Bush administration
under a Republican Congress
so where is the scandal
under President Obama

Republicans in Congress
passed a bill
given more power to The Executive Branch
over the other branches of government

A Republican Attorney General
under the Bush administration
was responsible for Fast and Furious
trading Guns for Drugs

So why question Eric Holder
about Fast and Furious
go grill that Attorney General
that was appointed by George Bush

The Republican Control Congress
asked a Phone Company
to turn over phone records
to check private citizens phone accounts

Trying to manufacture a scandal
because you have a problem
accepting Barack Obama
as your President in America

Public Service Announcement For Elvis Fans In The Building

Littler Richard and Chuck Berry
were the architects of Rock and Roll
not a poor White Man
from a dirt city in Mississippi

Who learned how to play
Delta Blues from Black Musicians
listen to Gospel Singers
that's the reason he sounded black

A Record Company from the fifties
had radio stations play his records
people bought the records
without knowledge that he was white

Now the same thing is happening
with Rap Artists of today
pushing the White Detroit Rapper
while minimizing the Black Chicago Rapper

Yes! He's a pompous ass
don't take his genius for granted
when an Ex-President's conscious suffers
that Rapper has relevant

He interrupted a White Singer
Press crucified him in the Media
President called him a jerk
same one who should have guts

Black achievement taken for granted
White's must be the innovators
they never like true History
smacking them in the face

You see it on Television
see it in the Movies
Black's need White validation
before they are accepted

Too many Black Artists
fall into the trap too many times
it's the perception of black thinking
when they see dollar bills

Let them change for you
not the other way around
you'll never get respect
unless you demand respect

The Great Jim Brown # 32

Jim Brown was the greatest Running Back
whoever played the game
doesn't really matter
what the record book said

Lead the league in rushing
eight of nine years he played
average over a hundred yards
every game that he played

Had fifteen hundred yards
in a twelve game season
when they moved up to fourteen
had a eighteen hundred yard season

He was more than an Athlete
was a man for social change
stood behind Ali the boxer
when he resisted the Draft

You can talk about the great Running Backs
who played the game
but none were greater
than Running Back Jim Brown

Average over five yards
every time he touch the ball
he could run around you
as well as run through you

It took nineteen years
for a running back to break his record
couldn't do it in fourteen games
so they moved to sixteen games

Had Crips and Bloods
inside his own home
got them to organized a truce
to stop the killings in their hoods

He was a Movie Star
selected movies of high quality
but he always had time
to fight against Black Injustice

He form Amer-I-Can
for Inmates and former Gang Members
to keep them from going back
inside the Prison System

If more Black Athletes
use their notoriety and fame
all Black People would benefit
instead of them showing off their wealth

Money Mayweather

You can call him chicken
you can say that he's scared
but Floyd Money Mayweather
calls all the shots

Why do Black Champions
with undefeated records
have to bow to the wishes
of Boxing Media and the Fans

Never do White Champions
get this kind of demand
they're the protected White Hope
or the shining Golden Boy

So if the Pac Man
doesn't submit to a blood test
then he doesn't get a taste
of seventy million bucks

The White Boxing World
doesn't like a Black Champion
dictating all the terms
of what fight it will be

Dale Robinson

Notice that he doesn't respond
to what the public said
he knows that the money
revolves around him

That's what really irritates
the Boxing Community at Large
they made not like it
but that's how the game is played

Pac won't submit to a Steroid test
Pac won't get seventy million bucks
then he can go back to fighting
those cheap tomato cans

You can call Mayweather a punk
he's laughing all the way to the bank
so all you White Promoters
smoke your Cigars and shut up

But that pisses them off
a Black Man with that much power
who seems quite contented
fighting twenty million dollar chumps

For The Tea Party

All you Tea Baggers
who think Obama's a socialist
you're the new Ku Klux Klan
without the sheets

The Rich say to you
keep being our distractions
after making our billions
we'll laugh in your faces

Socialize Healthcare
until that massive Heart Attack
one less person
to serve the tea

To all you Coffee Potters
it's not a Government takeover
you can't see any Black man
with any kind of power

The Rich say to you
keep being our distractions
after making our billions
we'll laugh in your faces

Government control Healthcare
until Incurable Cancer
one less person
to serve the tea

You should be in Wonderland
without Alice in the story
having tea with Mad Hatters
and the Marsh Hares

Or the Cats of Cheshire
with those goofy smiles
who know the subplots
of your stupid plans

Yes! all you Cup Juice Sippers
who talk of subsidize care
which some don't have
while others were dropped

You welcome Ms. Palin
to your lunatic fringe
so you can have legitimacy
instead of being call racist crack pots

This is all about race
not some Government control
that causes you to say vile things
about the negro in charge

Pissing Off The NRA

Ban Assault Rifles
Ban Military Grade Weapons
Ban the Semi Automatic Weapons
and the Automatic Weapons too!

You don't need a weapon
that shoots fifty to sixty rounds a minute
to protect your family
from the evils in the world

Just a simple thirty eight
or a forty five caliber pistol
that's all you need
to protect your family

You say Guns don't kill people
people kill people
tell that to the Parents of the six year old
who lost her life watching a movie

Then we have the Cowboys
who think they can hit a suspect in the crowd
not even being aware they might hit
an innocent bystander

Military Grade Weapons
are not meant to walk around with
their only adjective for their uses
is killing masses of people

They should only be used
for Target practice
at a Local Range in your area
not on America's streets

O! by the way
why not have a background check
to make sure you don't have
a criminal record

You don't want to do it?
what are you trying to hide!
you think someone will see something
that will deprive you from owning a Gun

If you want an Automatic Glock
first get it registered
then get training how to use it
before carrying it in the street

But it's not about the Second Amendment
it's about trying to justify
the perceived threat that comes
from Black People in America

We're Taken Back Our Country! What????

Conservative White Republicans feel
their Second Amendment is under attack
so they buy up all the guns
before the government restricts their sales

You need to read the First Amendment
in concurrence with the second
to get a clearer picture
on what rights you truly have

You talk of getting your government back
from a government taking your rights
without knowing the extent
how vast your government has become

First you must form a Militia
before you take up arms
that can't be abridged
from every citizen of America

But this not Seventeen Ninety
this is Two Thousand thirteen
if you think of trying that strategy
you'll be stop after a step

In the Seventeen Nineties
their were no Military Organizations
your local state Militias
were your Military Forces

In Two Thousand Thirteen
all four branches of the Military
are in all fifty states
along with thousands of Police Forces

In Two Thousand Thirteen
there are FBI field offices
in all fifty states
of these United States of America

There are CIA field offices
in all fifty states of America
and Homeland Security
in all fifty states of America

So all you wood beat Survive fools
and all you White Supremacist groups
would never stand a chance
against the full force of The United States

If the President of The United States decides
to take all weapons away from people
how is your Little Army
going to fight the juggernaut call America

And if you resist the Presidents orders
you'll be shot dead on the streets
like badly injured animals
mistreated by their masters

I'm Not A Racist

You said you're not a racist
then why open your mouth
if you have to justify
then you must be one

You say you get offended
when I call you a racist
if you try to justify
then you must be one

Then if you're not a racist
then why this talk about Obama
as trying to become Hitler
with a socialist agenda

It's not what you say with your mouth
but what you do by your actions
that determines if you're racist
or if you're really not

If you say you're not a racist
then why you say with your mouth
that you hope that he fails
or a white priest prays that he dies

I should be the one who's offended
as a black man in America
so don't give me your garbage
that you're the one oppressed

If you're not a racist
then why this racist talk
that you don't want this black man
talking to your white kids

Again not what you say
but what you do by your actions
that determines if you're a racist
or if you're really not

You're just a body who smiles
who tries to deny
that he's not really a racist
but in reality he is

You're one in a million
I see everyday
who plays like he's the victim
when he's a racist all the time

Dale Robinson

Revisionist History

Marian Anderson had no hard time
singing at Constitution Hall
it was because of racism
by the Daughters of the Revolution

The Civil War wasn't fought
because of State Rights
slavery was the issue
that started the war

You create your own History
to exclude the truth
so not to feel guilty
by the pain you inflict

Like putting every racial ethnicity
in the struggle for Civil Rights
when no race of people struggle
like Black People in America

From the Aborigines to the Indians
Central Americans to Africans
no people suffered more
than Black People in the world

Other races came voluntarily
to the continent of America
while Black People came in chains
to the continent of America

Where their faces were bashed in
like they were Emmett Till
or lynched by the Klan
to hang dead on trees

Whipped by racist Plantation Owners
until Black's comply to their wishes
Black Women being raped
because they were Slave Owners property

You want to exclude all that
to clear your own conscious
but until you face the truth
it's a wound that still festers

Like this bill that was past
to have a confederate Celebration month
that never even discusses
the history of slavery

As far as I'm concern
you have no rights at all
because you lost a bloody war
that lasted four years

When you surrender in a war
you give up all rights
to voice your opinion
or send bills to State Representatives

But you can't let the ghost go
of Civil War past
even thou you avoid the racist blueprint
you inflicted on a people

Now we have Radio and TV talk shows
that puke out the same racism
to raise the flames of hatred
to create a Race War

That can easily be created
with the Militias and hate groups
who really carry out the plan
with guns instead of microphones

From Planet Chaos To Earth

Hell was walking the streets
on the corner of Don't Give A Damn
everyone was afraid
that the world would end

Women were walking around
wearing just their pantyhose
while their breasts are bouncing free
in the cool spring breeze

Women cussing at each other
on the corner of Disrespect
using every racist epithet
when walking pass each other

Men were greeting each other
with racist epithets
while their jock strap cock pieces
conceal what you can only imagine

One race was blue
the other race was green
totally annihilating each other
because of racist hate

Destroyed each other
with every weapon you can imagine
people sliced in half
by their laser weapons

Anti Probe Gun weapons
destroyed five city blocks
one hundred fifty people
reduced to a pile of dust

Energy Particle Ray Guns
took all the electrical energy
from dead bodies
that once had life

Dead Talk Show Hosts
lay dead with microphones in their hands
at every Radio Station
all over the planet Chaos

People lay dead
inside bombed out buildings
people lay dead
on every street corner on Chaos

All this death on Chaos
because of racist hate
that's why I left the planet
in my spaceship to Earth

Chaos is just six million light years
from planet Earth
there was no future there
that's why I travel to Earth

But when I came to Earth
I knew their Future
arguments between the races
would lead to the same conclusion

Got back inside my spaceship
took off into space
still searching for a planet
that lives in total peace

The Republic (an) of Racist Stupidity

You say he's not American
he shows you his Birth Certificate
after it was shown
still you don't believe

You say it's not authentic
you say it's just a fake
you're not from The United States
but from The Republic(an) of Racist Stupidity

You say that he's a Muslim
he said he was a Christian
after he shows you his church
you still think he's a Muslim

You say he's got to be a Muslim!
because of his very name
you're not from The United States
but from The Republic(an) of Racist Stupidity

Call his health plan Obamacare
but offer no reasons why it's not good
just a bunch of stupid white people
who belong to The Republic(an) of Racist Stupidity

Then it's about his Education
he shows you his Diploma
his Diploma said he graduated
still you say it's not real

scared that he's smarter than you
so you denigrate his achievements
you're not from The United States
but from The Republic(an) of Racist Stupidity

You could have been like him
if you study harder in school
than relying on your connections
or your privilege way of life

You call him Mr. President
or just plain Obama
when you should show him respect
that he truly deserves

The Republic(an) of Racist Stupidity
is for people who are racist
who say outlandish statements
without showing you any proof

Stand Your Ground Against The Black Man

A White Man can shoot a Black Man
dead in the street
stand behind stand your ground
to get away with murder

There's a Stand Your Ground Law
in the state of Florida
that gave an excuse for a White Man
to kill a Black Teen name Trayvon

There's a Stand Your Ground Law
in the state of Texas
now White People can get away
with murdering Black Folks

There's a Stand Your Ground Law
in the state of Idaho
now White Supremacist have an excuse
to murder Black People

All because of a perception
that Black's commit all of the crimes
White's need to protect themselves
because Police don't do their jobs

But it's because of Budget Cuts
for all Police Departments in America
that put the fear in White People
for them to bare arms

There's a Stand Your Ground Law
in the state of Wyoming
not only you can kill Bears
but also make Black people extinct

So if you threaten White People
in the state of Kentucky
the same Stand Your Ground Law
give them the license to kill Black People

Bet if White People get killed
by Black People in those states
if they use Stand Your Ground Laws
White's would want them all repealed

What about West Virginia
What about Alabama and Mississippi
those three states
have Stand Your Ground Laws

At least Twenty Four States
have Stand Your Ground Laws
with another five states
in the process of passing the law

So if you're a Black Person
who live or visit those states
don't appear to be a threat
or you'll in a grave like Trayvon

Voting Rights! Not A Racial Entitlement!!

Justice Scalia said Voting Rights
amounts to a Racial Entitlement
and Congress is to afraid
to dismantle Voting Rights

Justice Sotomayor said if that were the case
what about Shelby County Alabama
where two hundred forty case
involved some form of voting suppression

Then we have Justice Thomas
Smiling and Laughing with other justices
while Justice Roberts philosophize an explanation
why Voting Rights should be abolished

It's true race relations
has improved over fifty years
but a more sophisticated form of racism
still resides in America

Look at the two thousand Election
Votes weren't counted down in Florida
that cause George Bush to become President
instead of Al Gore

You want more evidence
look at the two thousand four Election
where people in Ohio stood in line
where they were suppressed and disenfranchised

Want more evidence
how about this two thousand twelve Election
where thirteen states
have new voter ID Laws

Laws that became law
three to four months before the Election
while Civil Rights organizations
had to rush to make sure people had the proper paperwork

So you see things have improved
but we still have far too go
to achieve true equality for all
to have Voting Rights to be dismantle

Church Of The Ungodly Racist

If the church doesn't stand up
and choose responsible leaders
then the people of God
should go straight to hell

This is not trying to be Christian
it's about racist hate
because the President of The United States
has a black face

From one channel to the next
it's the same racist crap
racist disguise themselves
as Godly Christian servants

Trying to use bible verses
to justify themselves
making people of color
feel that they're the ones ungodly

The oppress weren't ungodly
it was the ones who were the oppressors
who's wealth was more important
than serving God above

Most of them are White
with their racist congregations
trying to get the world
to listen to this poisonous hate

Religion for America
as long as you are White
all foreigners of every race
are shown out the door

It's your fault Middle Class
for being selfish and greedy
that caused the ethic morals of America
to be in this financial mess

Mixing politics and religion
to create racist resentment
aimed straight at the President
because his face is black

This is all about White Men
who don't like the idea
of a Black Man with intelligence
telling them what to do

Recycle Racism In A Can

A filth rich Billionaire Playboy
wants to march on Washington
so White Supporters of Obama can laugh
and call him a Jackass

A seventy something burned out Fox Commentator
said the President is not a traditional American
because he wants to make America
better for all people in this land

This is not the nineteen sixties
it's two thousand twelve
you been declared obsolete
time for you to be replaced

A Radio Talk Show Host from Clear Channel
creates delusions of grandeur
to get people to believe
that we're close to a Race War

Finally we threw out those crazy Tea Partiers
who put the Republican Party through hell
to get them to become more Conservative
to induce fear of Racist Hate

This is not the Cuban Missile Crisis
it's the diversity of our Country
that doesn't want the smell
of recycle racism in a can

Old White Males who live in America
are quickly becoming an Endangered Species
maybe in the next ten years
none of them will be around

Because you can't depend on your Offspring
who were exposed to different cultures
that see you as Old Obsolete Racist Bigots
who are out of touch from reality

This is the Second Decade
Of the Twenty First Century
Who want to move away
from this stupidity known as hate

No Black People showed Up

Black's complain that no one's interested
in their cultural history
but when a movie about Tuskegee Airmen appears
no Black People bother to show

But we can show up
when a black man wears a dress
buck dancing and clowning around
while acting like a buffoon

Where are the stories
about Egyptian Engineers and Educators
but when a movie about them comes out
no Black People bother to show

But we can show up
to see a bunch of Aunt Jemima's
told by a white women
to get black people's sympathies

What about a movie
about Crispus Attucks
that will never be made
because black's won't show up

What about a movie
about the life of Frederick Douglass
that will never be made
because black's won't show up

Lucas put up forty million
to make an Authentic Black Movie
and added another fifty million
to distributed it in movie theaters

We have enough Black People
in the movie industry
Black's couldn't come up with a hundred million
to make Black Historical Cinema?

No movies about Garrett Morgan
no movies about Eliza McCoy
only movies about Black People
who demean their own race

A View From The Mirror

I'm just as pissed off
as Bill Cosby was
when talking of the state
of my people today

Pull up those pants!
from off your ass!!
then listen to the Teacher
in the classroom

Stop listening to Rap Gangsta
that fills your ears
you fool are making Rap Stars
rich from your pockets

You need to stop cursing
on the Buses and Subways
you're just an embarrassment
to the Black Race

What about those Flash Mobs
who were stealing in Stores
the ones in Philadelphia
were all Black Folks

Beating up innocent folks
stealing their valuables
this isn't the results of Racism
it's just simple Assault

Having knowledge in the classroom
is not trying to be White
go talk to all the Dropouts
they'll tell you the truth

Forget about going to the Military
it's just too technical for you
can't be all you can be!
you simply can't even read!!

Your hero's should be Egyptian Masters
not dead Rap Stars
who were the Architects of the World
not in the Studio spitting Majestic Flows

Your foolishness needs to stop
so we can be great again
the ones who are the most powerful
are the ones who are educated

So I don't give a damn
if Black People are mad at me
it's time for the truth paddles
to put pain between your ears

Dale Robinson

America The Contradiction

No Country like America
freedom to do what you like
then why suppress the citizens
their right to cast their votes

No Country like America
the best food and clothes
all the clothes are made somewhere else
while shipping our food overseas

No Country like America
you can always get a job
then why close all the factories
and outsource jobs overseas

There's a serious contradiction
going on in our land
the hypocrisy is self evident
but we act like it doesn't exist

Making Billionaires out of people
at the expense of thousands of workers
who no longer can support their families
because all the jobs are gone

Subsidize Healthcare in other Countries
Countries invest in the best Education
but right here in Old Glory
Education is dumb down

So Children can no longer read
White Supremacists reinvent History
now we have school children
calling Easter Island statues Dumb! Dumb!

No Country like America
the racism is so beautifully thick
we have advances in technology
while our minds are trapped in the fifties

Where ordinary people go to jail
for failure to pay their taxes
while Billionaires Thurston Howell's
avoid paying any taxes at all

We represent freedom and democracy
it's just a contradiction of terms!
freedom if you're one percent
and homeless jobless streetwalkers for everyone else

Dale Robinson

Post Racial . . . . What?

Intelligent black elites
In so call post racial America
No excuses black masses
For using race as an excuse

Tell that to that Black Professor
Arrested at his home
Even though a Doctorate at Harvard
To white policemen another nigger

Young black collegiate
In so call post racial America
No excuses black children
For using race as an excuse

Tell that to those kids in Philly
Who couldn't swim in a crowded pool
When club members couldn't handle
The color of black skin

Blacks criticizing other blacks
When they disagree with Obama
For not going to the conference of racism
To present his case against colonialism

Tell that to the Ivory Coast
Whose coffee still belongs to France
Or those lands down in Zimbabwe
That colonial whites still own

Put post racial America to bed
That concept doesn't exist
A Black Ivy League Professor
And those Philly black kids can confess

Black intellectuals are you awake
To what's going on in America
If white racist have a chance
They'll shoot black people dead in the streets

Your education means nothing
Your money means nothing
Not the possessions that you own
Can insolate you from racist hate

They see you all as educated Negroes
That need to be put back in their places
If they can't win with their mouths
They'll let their guns end the arguments

In this age of Obama
This post racial generation
It's a twilight zone existence
That doesn't really exist

It's right before your eyes
If you're willing to take a look
A reality that blacks face
On a daily bases

Made In America

In stylize America
there are no Black People
and the stench of racism
never really existed

In stylize America
blacks only had a place
if they were Chauffeurs Butlers and Maids
or other acts of buffoonery

So when I see Black People
buying into American stylization
my heart sinks to my stomach
and I simply shake my head

It's Saturday morning cartoon fiction
created in the thirties
a sanitize version of America
without the problems of the world

Like the back lots of Hollywood
with clothes to dress up in
stories created and derived
out of some ones imagination

In stylize America
there is no point of view
they subjectively make you think
the way they want you to think

It has no social conscious
no purpose for any one's life
only fills the camera time
with the images of illusion

Only causes confusion
in the head of an intelligent mind
and hides the real meaning
of what truly is American made

Culturally White Out Condition

You bleached out your black skin
To look more white
It's not about beauty
It's called cultural conditioning

Bleached out your kids skin
To make them more white
You stop bleaching their skin
When they get the best grades

What psychological damage
Have you done to your kids
Only way to good grades
Is to become more white

Just damaged goods
No longer a threat
To the white power structure
That just destroyed your mind

Light skin black people
Never worry about that problem
They change their hair and looks
To look more European

Some use chemical peels
To bleach out their skin
Making themselves more acceptable
To the white world

If you can't afford the chemicals
You get the white make up
So you don't suffer the indignities
Of being a black person

This form of racism
Is called self hatred
That's more dangerous
Than a bullet to the head

A former Baseball Player
For the past two years
Took a rejuvenation drug
To bleach out his own skin

A two year progression
To bleach out his skin
Once he was a black man
Now a culturally condition white man

From Condition to Reconditioning

Black was for the bad guys
White was for the good guys
this is what you're taught
while watching movie westerns

White moves first
Black moves next
this is what you're taught
while you play a game of Chess

The trappings are still there
in this suppose Post Racial World
they engross you in foolishness
to take you away from racial issues

Black's are always villains
White's are always heroes
White's plant the seeds of self hatred
from the time you are born

All have to be recondition
to know that racism still exist
all must be recondition
that White Supremacy never left

White man on a vine
swinging though the jungle
knows more about Africa
than the natives of the land

White Superman stands in front
of the American Flag
fights for truth and justice
for the American way

Banks are control by White's
your Military is control by White's
open both of your eyes
and see the world around you

White's control the Stock Exchange
they control the Network News
anything that talks of race
gets pushed to the background

Racism is now global
all the riches of the world
are mostly in countries
that are dark in complexion

Religious Humanism

Yes! I believe in God
Not this man made variety
Who praises God above
While vaporizing the world

Heaven stockpile of weapons
Without the love of God
Where your pictures of the God figure
Is one showing megatons

Yes! I believe in God
Not this man made variety
Who praises God above
While profiting off humanities needs

Heaven filled with supplies and cures
Without the love of God
Where your pictures of the God figure
Is the sign of the dollar bill

You play God the fool
While getting your gospel on
If God came down tomorrow
The foolishness would be at an end

Yes! I believe in God
Not this man made variety
Who praises God above
As long as they are the same race

Heaven filled with hatred
Without the love of God
Where your pictures of the God figure
Is pictured as one race

The hypocrisy of religious leaders
Who teach us the words of God
That are only in for it
To make a profit for themselves

Not fighting against injustice
Only to build their Mega Churches
So people can only see them
As some form of a God figure

Black Mega Church Preachers

Black Mega Church Preachers
who made a billion dollars
the prosperity of your ministry
is the upliftment of your race

Give a hundred million to God
eight hundred ninety nine to the people
that money can be used
to help all the black race

Take eight hundred ninety nine million
help people pay their mortgages
take some of those millions
so children can have the best education

Black Preachers give up some millions
to find the cure for Cancer
give more of your millions
to correct the problems of Diabetes

Instead of prosperity ministries
and building acres of Mega Churches
give people all of your money
take one million for yourself

Hundreds of millions of dollars
can help Black Children go to college
hundreds of millions of dollars
can create jobs for black adults

Black People passing out pamphlets
saying do you believe in God
Brother! it's time for you
to become saved

But do these black people
really believe in God
or is it just an act
to enrich themselves in wealth

Black Preachers in the pulpit
go into convulsive fits
to get people to realize
that they need God in their lives

But do these same Black Preachers
really believe in God
or is it to try to justify
the money they get for themselves

Brother World! You don't believe in God
Black Preachers would you help your people
give to your black masses
instead of putting it in your pockets

A Vote Of No Confidence

Obama tells African Nations
Stop using colonialism as an excuse
For the reason your nations
Are still impoverished today

Let me present my evidence
Of the after affects of colonialism
Why countries can't profit
From poverty today

You have the country of Cote d' Ivoire
Who's cash crop is coffee
Even thou it's independent
Coffee profits belong to France

Because of Coffee contracts
Drawn up hundreds of years ago
That are still valid today
Even thou they're independent

You have a country call Zimbabwe
Use to be called Rhodesia
That occupied African black lands
By the barrel of the gun

Had their guns pointed at them
Forcing them to sign contracts
Now they're independent
But white's still own their lands

Want more evidence President Obama
Our own history is stained in blood
But our brand of colonialism
Is called Manifest Destiny

Seventh President Andrew Jackson
Signed the Indian Removal Act
That allows the American Government
To remove Indians from their lands

If the Indians did not obey
Government troops were sent in
To remove the Indians quietly
Or shoot them dead where they stand

When America has a problem
With a country in the world
Our government uses covert action
To place a leader to their liking

Every part of Africa
Was robbed of its national resources
Leaving their countries all but barren
When they were granted their independence

The second wave of colonials
Were the three superpowers
Who took Uranium and Plutonium
To produce their nuclear bombs

Now white's have attitudes
When black's talk of reparations
That we earned by working the fields
Of racist white slave owners

President Obama why are you afraid
To show the world that you're black
And expect for me to vote for you
After the end of a four year term

Special Education

You know they're not college bound
You know they're not learning in school
But no one seems to process that
When money is sent elsewhere

Don't tell me I'm not doing enough
For my child to achieve in life
When I take my child to Baltimore
To get the help that you don't give

Have to set up insurance accounts
Set up checking accounts
To take care of her basic needs
When I'm no longer around

Have to think of setting up a will
If I die at any time
This is the life of a parent
Who has a disabled child

They have the nerve to say to us
We're not doing enough for our kids
When we're doing all we can
To make sure there's a place for them to live

You don't care for the disabled
Warehouse them in school
Just sitting in a classroom
Treating them like fools

Autism sitting with Cerebral Palsy
Spine a bifida with the Mentally challenged
While teachers with no experience
Sit with their hands in the air

You have no money to spend
To get a specialist for every problem
But the money can only be used
For the occupation of another country

You say they're capable of learning
You give them Math and Science
Which they can't possibly do
Because of the damage of their brains

Then you fault all of the parents
Say you're not doing enough for your child
When you show all of the evidence
That these kids need special help

So when we die tomorrow
Someone will take our place
To give them all the love
When we're no longer around

Saga Of The Black Artist

What's wrong being a Black Artist
ashamed of who you are
so you can make more money
from every culture in the world

When it always comes to us
we hide who we are
so we can be acceptable
with the rest of the world

What's wrong being a Black Artist
don't give me that crap!!
about trying to have diversity
when your motives are on the wealth

When it always comes to us
we hide who we really are
we're made to feel ashamed
if we're not part of the crowd

I'm not ashamed to be call
just a Black Artist
that presents his viewpoints
to the public at large

Not changing my subject matter
for the approval of the crowd
if they don't like what I'm about
then they can go straight to hell!!

Why don't we have self love
for who we really are
without changing our identity
because they think we're too black

Or Black artists who are affected
by the disease of cultural conditioning
seeing value in other cultures
while devaluing their own selves

I'm proud of who I am
shout it loud to the world
if I can't have my identity
then you can keep all of the gold

Democracy to Plutocracy

There are Four Hundred Billionaires
who live in this land
that make more money
than the population of nine states

But you think these Billionaires
have enough money
not by their thinking
they just want more wealth

Their Lobbyist are The Tea Party
who are paid millions of dollars
to convince Congress People
that Social Programs are entitlements

Destroy Social Security
that has trillions of dollars
give it to the two percent
in the form of Tax Cuts

Destroy Medicaid and Medicare
that has trillions of dollars
give it to the two percent
in the form of Tax Cuts

Destroy the Retirement System
that has trillions of dollars
give it to the two percent
in the form of Tax Cuts

While poor people in this country
are reduced to Slave Labor
going to country to country
overseas as cheap labor

Gave all our tax money
to bailout the Banks
now Banks won't give us credit
that we pay in taxes

Gave all out tax money
to bailout Corporate America
but they don't want to use it
to create Jobs in America

Hypocrites talk of Fiscal Responsibility
don't raise the Debt Ceiling!
but you raised it seven times
to give Tax Cuts to the wealthy

So all this talk
about government waste
is only a smoke screen
to keep rich people rich

Dale Robinson

The United States Of Whatever

Nutty Congressional Tea Partiers
want the Government to default
that's not going to happen
because of the Presidential Pen

If we can't pay back China
their two trillion dollars
then we will be called
The United States of China

If we pay back China
and can't pay back the Japanese
then we will be called
The United States of Japan

It will be that way
if we can't pay back a trillion
to the Japanese Government
if we default on our loans

If we can't pay back Saudi Arabia
their billions of dollars
then we will be called
The United States of Saudi Arabia

It will be that way
if we default on our loans
that we owe to other countries
who keep America strong

If we can't pay back Europe
it's billions of dollars
then we will be called
The United States of Europe

Europeans with their Euro
is keeping us afloat
both of our countries
depend on each other's prosperity

If we can't pay back The Caribbean Banks
their billions back
then we will be called
The United States of The Caribbean

So we can't just simply default
on what we owe to the world
until we find another answer
we have to raise the Debt Ceiling

All because of Republicans
who spent money like drunken sailors
that left a debt of ten trillion
before Obama became President

Tapped

Ringinginging
who's this on the phone
it's the NSA!!
who just tapped your phone

Your privacy has been invaded
we know where you are
you're not that far away
from our phone lines

Ringinginging
who's this on the phone
it's the CIA!!
who just tapped your Internet

Your privacy has been invaded
we know where you are
when you plug in your Computer
we know what it's for

First it was Congress
now the phone company
what's next on the agenda
your precious right to vote

Ringinginging
who's this on the phone
it's the FBI
who just contacted your job

Your government wants to find out
what groups you belong
to find out if your opinions
are subversive at all

The only thing left to do
is leave American soil
so you don't have to fear
about the things you say

Leaving so soon!!
is there anything to hide??
maybe we'll detain you
for further questioning

You say the world has changed
after September 11
all based off of lies
to take my freedoms away

Ringinginging
who's this at my door
it's the Uniformed Secret Service
to place me under arrest

We're arresting you for questioning
the government too much
instead of letting government
take your civil liberties away

Consequents Of Choice

A black R&B male singer didn't cause the death
of a black female R&B singer
it was the choices she made
that cause her own demise

It's like obese people who say
Fast Food cause them to become fat
when it's their responsibility
not to eat in those Restaurants

If someone told you to jump a cliff
would you jump that cliff
you would die like they would
in the very same matter

People make too many excuses
when they make the wrong choices
and blame other people
for the mistakes they made

When it comes to life and death
that choice could be your life
and the blame should be placed
squarely on your shoulders

You go to dance clubs
where alcohol and drugs are served
it's the choice of the individual
which road to choose

There are Record Company Parties
where alcohol and drugs are served
it's the choice of Recording Arts
which road to choose

There are Hollywood after parties
where alcohol and drugs are served
it's the choice of Movie Stars
which road to choose

So it wasn't murder
like the Tabloid said
it was her own self destructive behavior
that cause her own demise

So if someone tells you
to go out and kill someone
he will be charged as an accessory
while you be charged with murder one

You'll fry in the electric chair
for being a dumb behind
an all because of a decision
that was made by an individual

Dale Robinson

The United States of The Third World

No more Gold Standard
making worthless paper
backed by foreign currencies
to keep America strong

While this is going on
ideologies fight among themselves
while the ten ton debt truck
is heading straight in their path

Six Hundred Billion in chlorophyll paper
was added to the federal reserve
backed by foreign currencies
to add to our debts

We're just a paper tiger
the laughing stock of the world
expecting the world to stop their growth
so America can catch up

Want to know another joke?
where do we get our money for fighting wars
we borrow other people's money
to play the tin soldier

Last days of a dying empire
selling off the American Dream
going to the highest bidder
until America is no more

Selling off all of the businesses
selling off all of the Automobile plants
forecloses homes on the stock market
until America is no more

billionaires getting tax cuts
to store in foreign Bank Accounts
so when America dies
they board a plane to Switzerland

Seven Hundred Billion in chlorophyll paper
for two percent of the wealthiest people
adding to our debt
that we already have

Want to hear another joke?
where do we get our money to run our country
giving billions in bad debts
to receive credit from other nations
U.S.A Police of The World—October 20, 2011
You're the head of NATO
the UN Security Force
when there's trouble in the world
we dispense our brand of justice

In the nineteen thirties
Saudi Arabia had large oil deposits
but no adequate equipment
to get it out the ground

So we gave them the equipment
to get it out the ground
in return for the favor
we get twenty five percent

They don't have an Embassy
on Embassy road
their Embassy is down the street
from the Kennedy Center

In the nineteen fifties
Iran tried to nationalize their oil
America helped the English
to get rid of their leader

By a misinformation campaign
telling people how bad he was
when they got rid of Mosaddeq
America put The Shah of Iran in his place

A brutal dictator
who threw a million people in jail
for speaking out about his brutality
and the murdering of his people

Now we come to Qaddafi
who was killed just today
took genocide by his hands
for America to intervene

The French and English
were the colonial powers
when their oil reserves were threatened
they got help from America

OPEC oil reserves
were threaten by Qaddafi
along with his genocide
NATO was sent to kill him

Qaddafi was no angel
sent people to bomb a plane over Lockerbie
responsible for killing American troops
in a discotheque in Germany

But you have to ask the question
would OPEC even care
about the people of Libya
if there was no oil in the ground

Masters Of The World

Think the President of America
is the most powerful person in the world
then you're naïve
want to know the truth

This is bigger than any President
or leaders of other Nations
it's a race for all natural resources
to become master of the world

Collecting all the Gold
and the Silver in the world
collecting all the Platinum
and Diamonds around the world

Oil Barons who'll pay for wars
that kill innocent people
to collect all the Oil
to make themselves richer

Don't forget about the Uranium
and Plutonium buried in the ground
that produce the Nuclear Bombs
that destroys the whole world

The Titanium and Tungsten
that build the ships and planes
it's controlling all the resources
to become master of the world

A hand full of Billionaires
from around the world
who would stop at nothing
to become master of the world

Doesn't matter if it's Coffee
or Rubber from jungle trees
if it's a commodity to make billions
people will try to conquer

Collecting all the Sugar
collecting all the Cocoa
that's why countries like Cote d' Ivoire
can't benefit from their resources

It's a game that's played
by every Billionaire in the world
a race to see who'll become
the master of the world

Intelligent To Know Better

Have a Black disabled child
Whom I worry about the future
She's a fifteen year old Black girl
With the mentality of a five year old

Midrange retardation
With an IQ in the forties
Still hasn't progressed
Thank God she hasn't regressed

What will be her future
In this technological outsource
That only thinks you're useful
If you make money overseas

Don't need your off colored jokes
Saying you bowl like a special needs child
My child pieces puzzles together
But she also likes to bowl

If government doesn't care for normal people
What of the disabled ones
Will they become exterminated
Because they serve no useful purpose

It's no joke to me
Just broke my heart in two
Seeing the leader of the free world
Express that joke on a talk show

What about the weak and huddle masses
You claim that you protect
All down the drain
To greedy people who don't care

America has truly ate its young
No more high school diploma jobs
Since you can't afford college
It's the military industrial complex

Still my daughter can't read
Doesn't write any sentences
What's left for her to do
In a country without regard

No one to protect her
When I'm dead and gone
Think on this one Mr. President
You're intelligent enough to know better

Baptized In The Kingdom

Emerge from the pool
to become a new being
in the service of God
new member in his Kingdom

But that doesn't mean
you keep on sinning
but if you do sin
you're forgiven threw the blood of Christ

So if someone tells you
you can be Baptized by sprinkling
tell them the only way to bury your sins
is by immersing the human being

Burying your sins
is like burying you at death
your body turns back to dust
while your soul ascends back to God

Listen to John's message
repent an be baptized
come to the pool
and become part of the family

So if someone tells you
you can be baptized by touching a forehead
you make God's work ineffective
so he never excepted you

Come on submerge your sin
time is growing short
to bury all of your sins
before the door close

Don't let the world tell you
about different ways of Baptizing
theirs only one method
to become saved from your sins

Just pick up a Bible
the answers are all there
immerse and bury your sins
emerge as a new being

The Marketing Of A Presidential Icon

A circus has come to town
Sideshow of the absurd
Like the wolf face boy
Beside the bearded girl

There were hand clappers for sale
So your bands wouldn't be cold
Barack hand puppets
For only ten bucks

There were T-shirts and hoodies
Caps with Obama's name
To keep the body warm
On those cold winter nights

I'm not against Barack
People need a souvenir
But don't you really think
This was way over the top

Halloween mask of Barack
Are going a bit too far
Don't need a plastic figurine
That said yes we can

Do we really need an image
Of Barack on earrings
Do we really need an image
Of Barack on a watch

Some vendors are opportunist
In it for the quick bucks Exploiting of the image
For the purpose of a profit

No problems with postcards
Or books for you to read
It's putting the image of Barack
On everything you see

What's the next thing you'll see
Barack's image on shoe polish
One day while going shopping
See his image on toothpaste

I'm not against Barack
Take a moment to think
Did you listen to the message
Or was it an item to collect

Globalization

Who's in control
not the President of The United States
it's Oil Executives and CEO's
who have all the power

They send their Lobbyist to Congress
to make deals with the government
so they can receive bailouts
at Tax Payers' expense

No matter if people die
on offshore Oil Rig explosions
as long as they get their billions
from the Oil in the ground

No one's gone to trial
no one's gone to jail
tell that to any person
who thinks you're a conspiracy theorist

Meanwhile the Gulf of Mexico
is covered in Petro Oil
people have lost their livelihoods
while CEO's are on their Yachts

Who's in control
not the President of The United States
it's the Military Industrial Complex
ran by Multibillionaires

They send their Lobbyist to Congress
to make deals with the government
to get the Military to fight wars
so Billionaires become richer

No one's gone to trial
no one's gone to jail
tell that to any person
who thinks you're a conspiracy theorist

Meanwhile American soldiers
who carry the Stars and Stripes
die because billionaires profits
are threaten by Dictators

That's what happen in Iraq
Saddam nationalize his Oil
and change his Oil revenues
from Dollars to Euros

America said! No you don't!!
you're not devaluing our Oil Profit!
how can we get rid of him?
let's tie him to AL-Qaeda!

No one's gone to trial
no one's gone to jail
and the band plays on
so Billionaires can rule the world

Now it's off to Afghanistan
to control their Natural Resources
there's Lithium in the hills
for us to profit on

If the Computerize Electronic Highway
goes totally black
will have all of the battery power
to still rule the world

Who has the most money
makes all of the rules
who has the most resources
is the one who rules the world

If you are a good person
it's not the things of earth
want to be a Godly person
then you must first reject the world

Relief Fund-Haiti

Instead of sending billions
to fight the war in Iraq
send the money
to the Haitian relief fund

Instead of sending billions
to fight the Afghan war
send the money
to the Haitian relief fund

It's the moral thing to do
not money for stupid wars
that leaves people without hope
of governing themselves

Instead of sending billions
to Banks and Brokerage Houses
send that money
to the Haitian relief fund

It gives you a sense of conscious
for the cause of justice
money that's not wasted
because you have the available fund

So don't listen to televangelists
saying they made a pack with the Devil
because they fought Colonial France
keeping themselves from being enslaved

Or a ditto head talk show host
saying why we need to do this
for we all ready do this
by paying taxes every year

It's money to buy food
to stop the malnutrition
it's money for medical supplies
for the badly injured

Money to buy water
for the dehydrated
money for all humanity
instead of senseless destruction

Quarterback Racism In The NFL

You need to stay in the pocket
to develop your game
so you can be of value
for the team that you're on

Need to learn how to slide
when you run outside
to avoid the big hit
that takes you out of the game

But you can get a concussion
when you're in the pocket
going through your progressions
with your eyes down the field

And what's this about
letting your Offensive Line protect you
to avoid unnecessary hits
that you don't need to take

But if that protection fails
you're still running for your life
trying to avoid that concussion
that will end your day

Dale Robinson

White Quarterback gets upset
Yells at his Offensive Coordinator
it's seen on Television
without no one saying a word

It must be a disagreement
between the two parties
they're trying to win the game
for the sake of the team

Black Quarterback gets upset
Offensive Coordinator must be getting him upset
not thinking about the team
only thinking about how he feels

It's affecting the way he plays
need to rethink who we start
better get the backup ready
just in case we need a change

So if you're a White Quarterback
you can stay out all night
get drunk at a Bar
ends up sober in jail

Don't let that be a Black Quarterback
doing the same thing
now they're questioning his judgment
wonder if he's right for the team

White Quarterbacks in the league
can deviate from the Playbook
are called a bunch of Geniuses
if it wins them the game

Black Quarterbacks in the league
who deviate from the Playbook
are condemn by their coaches
when they don't win them the game

Coaches took over the play calling
because their jobs are at stake
now Quarterbacks are now Robots
program by their teams

For White Quarterbacks
their aloud to be a little creative
but for Black Quarterbacks
you're not costing the coaches their jobs

Oil Knights of The Round Table (Twelve)

Kuwait is a member
of the OPEC Nation
America's ultimatum to Saddam
was leave in six months

When Saddam didn't move
they pushed him back to Iraq
before he left Kuwait
he bum some oil fields

Iraq is a member
of the OPEC Nation
Saddam changed his Dollar currencies to Euros
America went to war

It was about Oil Profits
Saddam had no connection to Terrorism
got people scared of Bin Laden
that was the big lie

Libya is a member
of the OPEC Nation
Qaddafi changed his Euro currencies to Dollars
America NATO went to war

It was for Oil Profits
not about Qaddafi's genocide
if Libya had no oil
Qaddafi would still be alive

Iran is a member
of the OPEC Nation
America's first contact
was close to sixty years

Maybe it's Israel's Security
Maybe it's Nuclear Weapons
If OPEC Oil is threaten
that will be the excuse for fighting war

They're two OPEC Nations
in the hemisphere of South America
Ecuador is very quiet
while Venezuela draws attention

Saudi Arabia is a member
of the OPEC Nation
It's our largest importer
of foreign oil

One reason why they get
a detachment of Secret Service
to protect their Embassy
across the street from the Kennedy Center

Four African Countries
are members of the OPEC Nation
Libya is one of them
Algeria is another

Youths were rioting
in the streets of Algeria but they have no freedom
while under the restrictions of OPEC

Nigeria and Angola
have had their own political unrest
not only they have OPEC
but their own corrupt politicians

UAE is a member
of the OPEC Nation
three were questioned on a plane
because someone was scared of Terrorist

Qatar is a member
of the OPEC Nation
they are not in the News
like the other OPEC Nations